enlightened polymer clay

Artisan Jewelry Designs
Inspired by Nature

Rie Nagumo

INTERWEAVE.
interweave.com

Enlightened Polymer Clay
Artisan Jewelry Designs Inspired by Nature
by Rie Nagumo

Copyright © 2006 Rie Nagumo

First published in Japan in 2006 by Ondori-sha.
© 2006 Ondori-sha

English edition produced and printed in 2011 by Graphic-sha Publishing Co., Ltd.
1-14-17 Kudan-Kita, Chiyoda-ku, Tokyo 102-0073, Japan

Copyright © 2011 Graphic-sha Publishing Co., Ltd.

This English edition was first published in the United States of America in 2012 by Interweave Press LLC
201 East Fourth Street, Loveland, CO 80537-5655
www.interweave.com

ISBN-13: 978-1-59668-634-2

10 9 8 7 6 5 4 3 2 1

Planning:	Rie Nagumo
Editing:	Chieko Takeuchi
Piece design and production:	Rie Nagumo
Technical collaboration:	Sachiko Kurimoto (CRAFT HOUSE CORP.)
Production collaboration:	Miyako Tanikawa, Anzu Nagumo
Photography:	Francesca Moscheni, Giampiero Lorenz
	Wataru Nakatsuji (P. 3, P. 36-40, P. 69-72)
Styling:	Tomomi Enai
Book design:	Tomoko Nawata, Miki Wakayama (L'espace)
Illustration:	Mitsuru Iijima
Coordinator:	Cristiana Ceci
English edition layout:	Shinichi Ishioka
English translation:	Headgs Design Plus
Production and management:	Kumiko Sakamoto (Graphic-sha Publishing Co., Ltd.)

Printed and bound in China

contents

What is the attraction of jewelry made by yourself?
To express individuality and create jewelry you truly love to wear.
This is my basic idea in making jewelry.

In this book, I introduce such expressions using polymer clay.

Through a process of trial and error involving kneading, mixing, flattening, rolling, pulling and cutting out with a mold, you will gradually gain a clear picture of what you want.

Polymer clay allows you to easily control and combine subtle shades of colors, and create thin and delicate or thin and long shapes.

With this material's great flexibility, you slowly become attracted to it, and before you know it you are captured by it.

Polymer clay has great potential as a material for accessory making, with its easy-to-form and diverse possibilities of expression.

I hope that this book will inspire your creative ideas and help you to make your own jewelry.

Rie Nagumo

◯ FLATTENING

Roll clay rhythmically
back and forth,
making it thick or thin
as you wish,
back and forth.

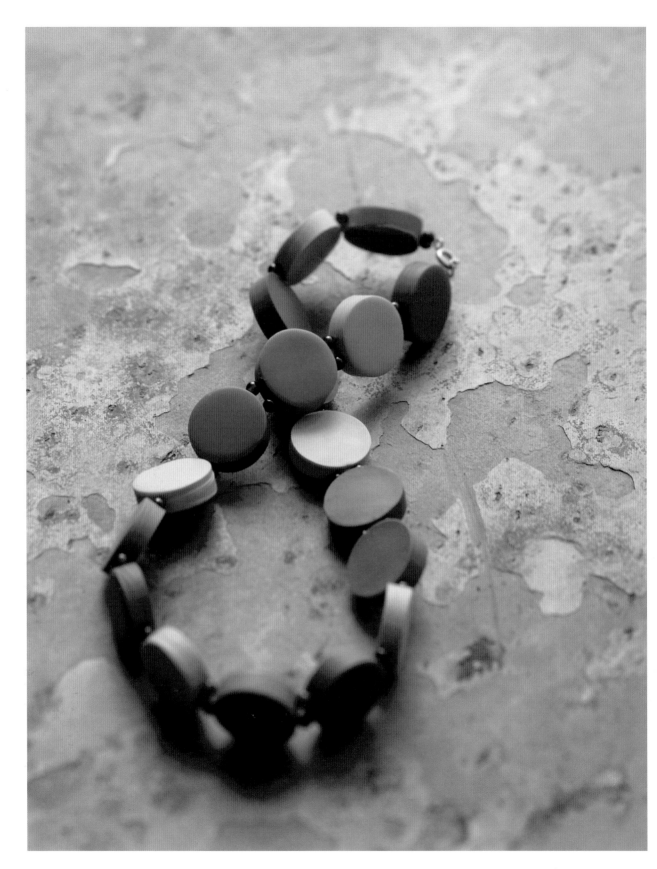

NO. 3 BROACH | How to make: page 44

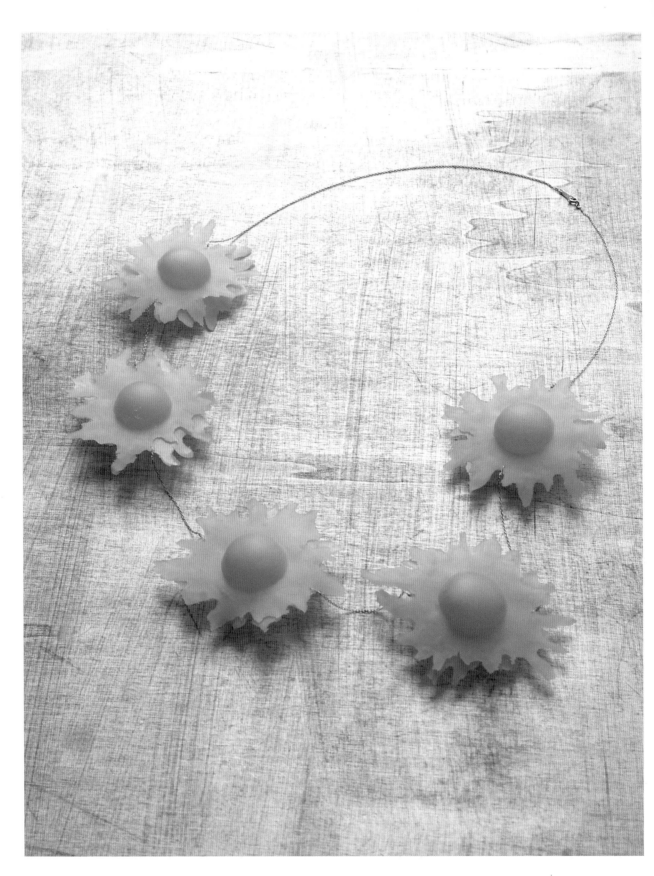

No. 5 Necklace | How to make: page 46

No. 9 Necklace | How to make: page 50

No. 11 Ring | How to make: page 52

ROLLING

Roll clay
in a circular motion,
roll it gently
until it forms a ball.
All you need is your hand

No. 12 Choker | How to make: page 53

No. 14 Necklace | How to make: page 55

No. 16 Necklace | How to make: page 57

How to make: page 58 | No. 17 Necklace

No. 18 Choker | How to make: page 60-61

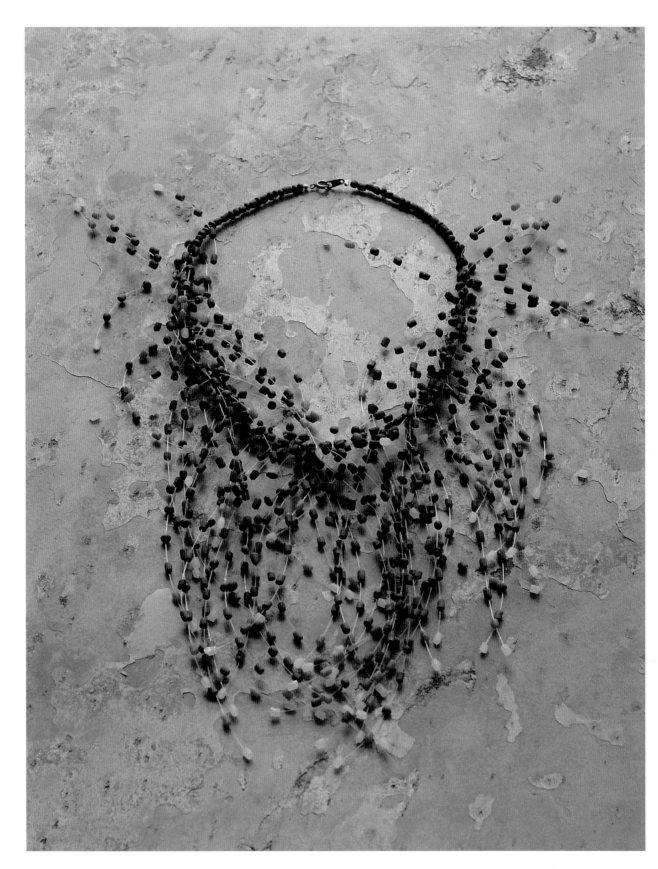

No. 21 Choker | How to make: page 59

No. 23 Pendant No. 24 Ring | How to make: page 63

◇ LAYERING

Layer different colored clay
to create your original color.
Once you have achieved it ,
the rest is all so easy.

No. 25 Necklace | How to make: page 64

No. 27 Necklace | How to make: page 66

TECHNIQUES

Polymer clay

Polymer clay is processed based on polymer polyvinyl chloride (PVC) into a workable clay-like material. Its plasticity allows hand kneading. Once heated in an oven, it hardens while keeping its unique elasticity. Its excellent processability is suitable for art objects and their specifications. It comes in a wide variety of colors (see p. 37) and you can create colors of your own by mixing them. Among them, FIMO CLASSIC and FIMO EFFECT have a resilient body which makes possible elaborate works, and durability which ensures stability of shape. Also, by polishing, you can produce the beautiful luster of natural stones or glass. With its pliability and elasticity, premo! is suitable for the creation of thin pieces. In this book, translucent type premo! Sculpey is used. Sculpey III is used for transferring design patterns.

FIMO CLASSIC and FIMO EFFECT
Each block consists of 8 segments
(approx. 7g or 0.25oz/seg)

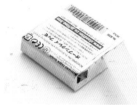

Open package
Place the package with the back side up, slit the upper edges on three sides with a slicer to open. It is recommended to keep the color number.

Cut into pieces
Place the slicer on a groove and cut straight down. Prepare the required amount based on the weight of each segment.

How to store
Wrap with a polypropylene (PP) sheet or keep in a PP container. Do not use polyvinyl chloride (PVC) container, or the clay will deteriorate and the container will be damaged. Paper is not suitable either, as the clay will dry up.

premo! Sculpey and Sculpey III
Each block consists of 4 segments
(approx. 14g or 0.50oz/seg)

BASIC PROCESS

Conditioning

This is to make polymer clay easy to form by kneading well. Use a polymer clay machine (or a dedicated pasta machine used for polymer clay).

1. Warming clay between your hands, make a rope, fold in half. Make a rope again by twisting. Repeat this twice.

2. Using a rolling pin, roll clay flat to a thickness so that it can pass through the machine.

3. Pass clay through the machine. Raise the setting on the dial, starting at No. 1, No. 2, and then to No. 3.

4. With the setting at No. 3, fold clay in half and pass through the machine. Repeat this 25 to 30 times. It is now ready for the color making or forming process (pp. 38–39).

When you don't have a machine.
1. Knead clay one segment at a time by hand until soft, while heating it to about 50°C or 122°F, using a hair dryer or incandescent lamp.

2. Using a rolling pin, roll clay flat, fold in half, turn sideways and roll again. Repeat until smooth. When making color (see p. 37), combine desired color clays and do the same.

How to use machine
The machine slots open based on the dial settings from No. 1 to 8. The larger the number, the narrower the slot opening, and thinner the clay.

★ Dial numbers and thickness of clay (after heating)

No. 1	2.6mm
No. 2	2.2mm
No. 3	1.8mm
No. 4	1.5mm
No. 5	1.2mm
No. 6	0.8mm
No. 7	0.7mm
No. 8	0.6mm

*Thickness may vary depending on the machine.

If clay is three times the thickness of the setting, it may become stuck. Be sure to make clay thinner gradually by raising the settings one at a time.

Color making

Make your own color by combining two or more different color clays using a machine or your hands. The following method is by machine.

1. Pass clay through the machine at setting No. 1. Cut clay into same size units using a clay cutter, to help you understand the amount of color clay to use for combining.

2. Cut each color in the same size. One segment (7g or 0.25oz) of FIMO CLASSIC/FIMO EFFECT equals one piece cut out with a clay cutter L, and four pieces with a clay cutter S; i.e. a quarter of a segment (a little less than 2g) equals one piece cut out with S.

3. Pass clay sheets together through the machine, fold in half and pass through again. Repeat this until the color becomes even and ready for forming (pp. 38–39).

Heating

Cure clay by heating in an oven.

First, place a piece of cardboard on the oven tray, and then add the clay pieces on a parchment paper. Place the tray in the preheated oven and heat for 30 to 60 minutes at 120°C to 130°C or 248°F to 266°F.

How to use an oven

★ When using PVC clay, be aware that it will start to melt at 150°C or 302°F and produce toxic smoke. Watch the temperature and provide good ventilation.

• Preheat the oven to 130°C or 248°F.
• Always keep an oven thermometer in the oven.
• Never use an oven toaster.

★ As the temperature setting may not be reliable depending on the oven, watch the actual temperature when heating clay.

★ Clay tends to become shiny at parts where contact is made with metal during heating. Avoid placing clay directly on the oven tray.

★ If the clay piece(s) is unstable, crunch the parchment paper beforehand.

Finishing

Polish the clay using a sandpaper, rotary tool, or varnish. Make sure that the clay is thoroughly cooled after heating.

1. Using waterproof sandpaper for the flat surface, and sanding sponge pad for the curved surface, polish while applying water. In both cases, start with a coarser grit.
Waterproof sandpaper: #400 → #1000 → #1200
Sanding sponge pad: super fine → ultra fine

2. Ensure the surface is smooth by touching with your fingers. Attach cloth buff to a rotary tool and lightly polish in a stroking motion.

When you want to have a shiny finish without polishing, make sure that the clay piece has thoroughly cooled, and soak it in varnish; or brush varnish on and let it dry naturally.

FIMO CLASSIC
Standard colors

0	White
02	Champagne
1	Yellow
15	Golden Yellow
17	Ochre
2	Red
21	Magenta
23	Bordeaux
29	Carmine
32	Light Turquoise
33	Ultramarine
34	Navy Blue
37	Blue
38	Turquoise
4	Orange
43	Fresh Pink
45	Dark Flesh
5	Green
57	Leaf Green
6	Lilac
77	Chocolate
9	Black
8026	FIMO Mix Quick

Clay for extra flexibility and smoothness

FIMO EFFECT

| 08 | Pearl |
| 11 | Metal Gold |

premo! Sculpey

| 5310 | Translucent |

This highly transparent clay produces a beautiful translucent effect.

Sculpey III

| 010 | Translucent |

 **Forming**

At this stage, you create a form or pattern suited to your design by rolling clay flat, into a ball, or layering.

FLATTENING

Use a rolling pin, while placing the thickness gauge strips on both sides. You can make the clay as thin as the thickness of the strips.

Use a rolling machine to produce an even thickness according to the setting.

Pull the edge of an evenly flattened piece with fingers, to partially vary the thickness.

Grate clay, lump together and roll flat to produce a unique cracked texture.

Roll together more than two colored clays to produce a marble pattern.

At setting No. 8, place the clay on parchment paper and pass through the machine. This will produce an ultra-thin piece of clay without tearing.

ROLLING

Roll with a finger, or the palm if the piece is big, to produce a nice sphere.

Place fingers as shown and roll back and forth to produce cord or needle shape clay.

Place the clay ball in a clay gun and extrude to produce a thin cord, the size of the gun orifice.

How to make a wood-grain pattern.

LAYERING

1. Cut out the specified color clay into the given number of sheets with a square clay cutter.

2. Layer the sheets while avoiding air bubbles, and press down with fingers to make it thinner.

3. Cut in half and laminate two sheets into one rectangular block. Press down with both hands and make it thinner as in 2. Repeat a few times.

4. Place the clay on a tile with its wood-grain side up. Fix well and slice thinly in a scooping manner with a slicer.

5. Place the sliced chip on the base clay with its back side up (which contacted the slicer blade), and smooth the surface with fingers.

How to make a wood-grain pattern with gold leaf.

1. Cut out clay to the given number of sheets, alternate the layers of white clay and gold leaf, finishing with black clay. Apply gold leaf gently using a dry brush.

2. Cut into four blocks. Use a thick ruler or the like to press each cut edge down so that the top black layer sinks into the layers of white clay and gold leaf, creating a moiré pattern consisting of white, gold and black lines. Join the four blocks back together into one piece at their moiré sides.

3. Slice off the top black clay surface to expose the wood-grain–like pattern i.e. mixture of white, gold and black. Slice thinly in a scooping manner as shown above. Place the sliced chip on the base clay with its back side up, and smooth the surface with fingers.

Transferring patterns

This is a method to re-transfer a pattern to clay which has been copied onto paper by a black-and-white copy machine, which uses black toner. Use Sculpey III (Translucent) for clay without conditioning. Cut the clay into 3mm thick pieces, and pass through the machine. Repeat, each time raising the setting on the dial, starting at No. 6, then No. 7, and No. 8. At No. 8, pass the clay through together with parchment paper to produce an ultra-thin piece.

1. Transfer a pattern onto a piece of white paper, and place on the clay printed side down. Apply a good amount of ethanol over the paper using a soft brush.

2. Make the surface warm by rubbing with a finger. Repeat when dry. Repeat twice more.

3. Lift paper to check. If the pattern is successfully transferred, remove the paper. If not, apply more ethanol with the brush. Cut out the printed part of the clay and place on the base clay with the printed side down.

Combining with a fine silver ring

Make a ring with fine silver clay. Use a metal clay ring maker mold and it will be very easy.
This is a tool to form a ring based on the mold principle.

Silver clay

PMC3 (Mitsubishi Materials Corporation) and Art Clay Silver 650 (Aida Chemical Industries Corporation Ltd) products are well-known as fine silver clays. It is a clay-type precious metal consisting of fine silver powder, water, and binders. You can form it just like other modeling clay, and after drying and firing, you will get 99.9% silver. Clay type (left) and paste type (right).

Ring maker molds

These ring maker molds consist of a top and base with a groove where they meet. Insert silver clay in the mold, and you can make a ring in the form of the groove. To prevent the clay from sticking, apply oil thinly to the inner surface before use.

Preparation

To make a half-round ring, place balled and slightly flattened disc-shape silver clay at the center of the base (left). To make a flat ring, insert a thickness guide of your choice in the base and add balled silver clay (right).

Molding

1. Attach the top piece to the base and hold sideways. Press the clay firmly with your index finger and fill in the groove through the center hole.

2. Confirm that the groove is completely filled with clay, and insert the cylinder in the center hole.

3. Press the cylinder further in while pressing the clay in from the other side also. Pressed from both sides, the clay will completely fill the groove.

4. Remove excess clay, push the cylinder out through the hole and carefully take the top piece off by twisting a little.

5. Dry the clay in the base (half-round ring) or in the thickness guide (flat ring), using a hairdryer (cold air), or naturally. When half dried, remove from the base or guide and dry completely.

Firing

Finish the surface using waterproof sandpaper, a half-round medium-grit file, and sanding sponge pad (left). Bore a hole with a pin vise or attach a silver key eye, as necessary before firing (center). Wrap ceramic tape around the shrinkage stopper, fit a ring, and place it on the PMC Mini Pan and fire using a portable stove (right). If the Mini Pan is not available, use a kiln tray for precious metal clay. You can also use an electric kiln.

Finishing

Polish as necessary based on your design, before combining with polymer clay part(s).
*Mirror finish (left): polish using in this order; stainless steel brush, sanding sponge pad, and silver polishing cloth. Satin finish (center): after mirror finishing, polish in one direction with the sanding sponge pad. Hammered finish (right): insert something hard in the ring, and hammer with a small jeweler's hammer and buff with the stainless steel brush.

HOW TO MAKE

NOTES

Symbols

L	M	S
40mm × 40mm	30mm × 30mm	20mm × 20mm

Clay cutter (square) in sizes; large (40mm or 1.6in sq), medium (30mm or 1.2in sq) and small (20mm or 0.8in sq).

Ⓛ Ⓜ Ⓢ
40mm φ 30mm φ 20mm φ

Clay cutter (round) in sizes; large (40mm or 1.6in Φ), medium (30mm or 1.2in Φ) and small (20mm or 0.8in Φ).

Volume references (rolled by polymer clay machine at setting No. 1):

FIMO CLASSIC/FIMO EFFECT
1 segment = 7g or 0.25oz = 1 pc cut out by L   [L] or 4 pcs by S

[S S / S S] 1/4 segment = a little less than 2g = 1 pc cut out by S

premo! Sculpey and Sulpey III
1/2 segment = 7g or 0.25oz = 1 pc cut out by L or 4 pcs by S
1/8 segment = a little less than 2g = 1 pc cut out by S

Amount of color clay when making color:

When indicated as 'small amount of', it is for reference only. A tiny amount can easily influence the final color. Find your choice of color while trying yourself.

Tip for conditioning:

When you condition a small amount of clay, it is easier if you do it while making it warm with your fingers

Precautions when heating:

When heating, watch the temperature carefully. Make sure to preheat the oven to 130°C or 248°F before inserting the clay and try to maintain this temperature. Polymer clay may discolor or burn at higher temperature as well as release toxic fumes. Use a home oven. Do not use an oven-toaster as the temperature tends to rise very suddenly. A microwave oven cannot be used either. Heat clay by placing it on a thick piece of paper or parchment paper, and then on the oven tray. Note: Please refer to accessories, tools, and firing tools at the end of the book.

Materials

Polymer clay [FIMO CLASSIC and premo!]

Olive-green:	1+1/5 segments of premo! 5310 (Translucent), 1/4 segment of FIMO CLASSIC 57 (Leaf Green), small amount of FIMO CLASSIC 0 (White) and 17 (Ochre)
Chrome-yellow:	1+1/5 segments of premo! 5310 (Translucent), 1 segment of FIMO CLASSIC 0 (White), 1/5 segment of FIMO CLASSIC 17 (Ochre), small amount of FIMO CLASSIC 1 (Yellow)
Sepia:	1+1/5 segments of premo! 5310 (Translucent), 1/5 segment of FIMO CLASSIC 77 (Chocolate), 1/3 segment of FIMO CLASSIC 0 (White), small amount of FIMO CLASSIC 9 (Black)

2 nylon wires (each 410mm or 17.3in long)

38 spacer beads (small)

1 clasp (spring ring and chain tab)

2 crimp beads

How to make

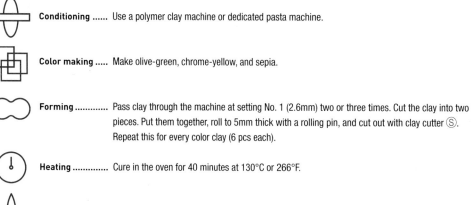

Conditioning ...... Use a polymer clay machine or dedicated pasta machine.

Color making ..... Make olive-green, chrome-yellow, and sepia.

Forming .... Pass clay through the machine at setting No. 1 (2.6mm) two or three times. Cut the clay into two pieces. Put them together, roll to 5mm thick with a rolling pin, and cut out with clay cutter Ⓢ. Repeat this for every color clay (6 pcs each).

Heating .... Cure in the oven for 40 minutes at 130°C or 266°F.

Finishing .... • Pierce the side of each clay bead in two places with a pin vise.
• String clay beads and spacer beads alternately on the nylon wire.
• Attach a clasp at the end of the wire and fix with crimp beads.

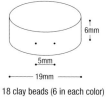

6mm

5mm

19mm

18 clay beads (6 in each color)

Materials

Polymer clay [FIMO CLASSIC and premo!]

Grey:	1+2/5 segments of premo! 5310 (Translucent), 1/2 segment of FIMO CLASSIC 0 (White), small amount of FIMO CLASSIC 77 (Chocolate) and 5 (Green)
Brown:	3/4 segment of premo! 5310 (Translucent), 2/5 segment of FIMO CLASSIC 77 (Chocolate), 2/5 segment of FIMO CLASSIC 02 (Champagne), small amount of FIMO CLASSIC 17 (Ochre)
Chrome-yellow:	1+2/5 segments of premo! 5310 (Translucent), 2/5 segment of FIMO CLASSIC 17 (Ochre), 2/5 segment of FIMO CLASSIC 0 (White), small amount of FIMO CLASSIC 1 (Yellow) and 02 (Champagne)
Vermillion:	3/5 segment of premo! 5310 (Translucent), 2/3 segment of FIMO CLASSIC 0 (White), 1/2 segment of FIMO CLASSIC 2 (Red), small amount of FIMO CLASSIC 17 (Ochre)

1 core material (72g or 2.5oz)

1 nylon wire (1.4m or 4.6ft long)

1 clasp (spring ring and chain tab)

2 crimp beads

Sculpey® Bake & Bond

Base

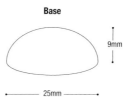

9mm

25mm

18 pcs

Preparation

Form core material e.g. cork modeling clay into half spheres, and dry to make bases (18 pcs). Chain stitch nylon wire to length of 450mm or 17.7in long.

How to make

Conditioning ...... Use a polymer clay machine or dedicated pasta machine.

Color making ..... Make gray, brown, chrome-yellow and vermillion.

Forming ....
- Form clay into a cylinder and grate using a coarse grater.
- Put the grated pieces together and pass through the machine at No. 2 (2.2mm) to produce clay with small cracks.
- Cover the round surface of the base. Trim off excess clay. Repeat this for each color clay.
- Grate clay again using a grater, pass through the machine at No. 2, and cut off the ragged edge in a strip (see Illustration A).
- Combine two clay-covered bases by sandwiching the ragged edged strip (see Illustration B), using Sculpey Bake & Bond (later called the bond).

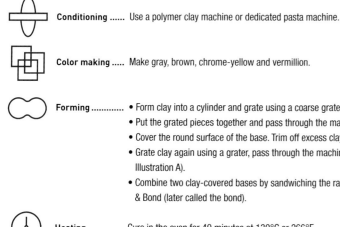

A

Heating .... Cure in the oven for 40 minutes at 130°C or 266°F.

Finishing ....
- Pierce a hole in the side of the clay with a pin vise, and pass chain-stitched nylon wire through it using a needle.
- Attach a clasp at the end of the wire and fix with crimp beads.

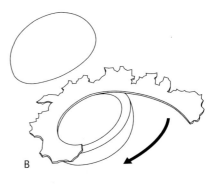

B

Materials

Polymer clay [FIMO CLASSIC and premo!]

Light-blue:	3/5 segment of premo! 5310 (Translucent), small amount of FIMO CLASSIC 34 (Navy Blue)
or;	
Yellow-green:	3/5 segment of premo! 5310 (Translucent), small amount of FIMO CLASSIC 1 (Yellow), 5 (Green) and 34 (Navy Blue)
or;	
Salmon-pink:	3/5 segment of premo! 5310 (Translucent), small amount of FIMO CLASSIC 77 (Chocolate) and 9 (Black)

45 artificial stamens (gold color)

1 brooch pin back

Sculpey® Bake & Bond

Base

5mm

15mm

1 pc

Flower center

5mm

8mm

1 pc

How to make

Conditioning ...... Use a polymer clay machine or dedicated pasta machine.

Color making ..... Make light-blue, yellow-green, or salmon-pink.

Forming .... Make petals:
- Pass clay through the machine at setting No. 3 (1.8mm) two or three times. Cut the clay into three pieces (25mm x 100mm or 1in x 4in).
- Press down with an ultra-hard fine-tipped burnisher (or clay modeling spatula) to make a fluted pattern (Illustration A). Cut into strips 5mm ~ 10mm wide.

Make the base, etc.:
- Form clay into a disk to make the base for the brooch (1 pc).
- Form clay into a half-sphere to make the center of a flower (1 pc).
- Arrange petals on the base neatly and place the flower center in the middle.
- Lightly pull and tear the edges of the petals with fingers (Illustration B).
- Insert stamens in the flower center.
- Attach a brooch pin with the bond, and cover the base of the pin back with a little bit of clay.

Heating .... Cure in the oven for 40 minutes at 130°C or 266°F.

Tips: You can also produce petals by making pleats on the flattened clay strip with a burnisher (or clay modeling spatula) and looping and attaching it to the base. Enjoy different variations by selecting stamens of your choice according to the petal color, e.g. those in plain black or with silver spangles.

A

B

Materials

Polymer clay [FIMO CLASSIC and premo!]

Semitransparent (petals):	3/5 segment of premo! 5310 (Translucent)
Black (anthers):	Small amount of FIMO CLASSIC 9 (Black)

5 brass wires (each 40mm or 1.6in long)

1 crimp bead (large)

2 pcs fabric for band (each 33mm x 640mm or 1.4in x 25.2in)

Sculpey® Bake & Bond

Preparation

Pull threads out from one edge of the fabric to make a fringe. Fold in three and stitch as shown on the right (Illustration A).

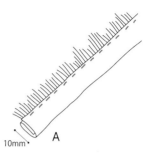

10mm   A

How to make

 Conditioning ...... Use a polymer clay machine or dedicated pasta machine.

 Forming .... Make petals:
- Pass the clay through the machine. Repeat, each time raising the setting on the dial, starting at No. 1 (2.6mm) and finishing at No. 7 (0.7mm) to gradually produce a thinner piece.
- Cut out two circular pieces, each with a diameter of 60mm or 2.4in and 70mm or 2.8in. Make the edges irregularly thinner with fingers to produce a wavy edge.

Make anthers:
- Make rice-grain sized balls with black clay (5 pcs). Apply the bond at the ends of the brass wires and insert into the balls.

Heating .... Cure in the oven for 40 minutes at 130°C or 266°F.

Finishing .... • Layer the two petals, make a hole in the center with a pin vise, and pass the brass wire through.
- At the back, bundle the wires with a crimp, and bend the ends. Wrap them with the fabric and finish with hemstitch.

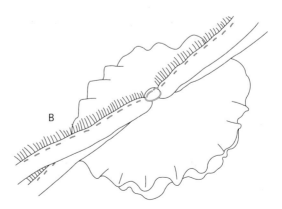

B

Materials

Polymer clay [premo!]

| Semitransparent: 6+1/4 segments of premo! 5310 (Translucent)

1 core material (40g or 1.4oz)

6 chains (total of length 585mm or 23in: 1 each of 210mm or 8.3in, 160mm or 6.3in, 75mm or 3in, 50mm or 2in, and 2 of 45mm or 1.8in)

1 clasp (spring ring and chain tab)

2 jump rings (small)

1 silver wire (400mm or 15.7in long)

Sculpey® Bake & Bond

Base

9mm

25mm (1in)

10 pcs

Preparation

Form core material, e.g., woodchip or cork modeling clay, into half spheres and dry to make bases (10 pcs).

How to make

 Conditioning ...... Use a polymer clay machine or dedicated pasta machine.

Forming .... • Pass the clay through the machine. Repeat, each time raising the setting on the dial, starting at No. 1 (2.6mm) and finishing at No. 7 (0.7mm) to produce a thinner piece gradually.
                                             • Cut out 10 sheets 100mm or 4.0in square. Cover the base with each sheet, press down, and tear off the edge with a finger (see Illustration A).

Heating .... Cure in the oven for 5 minutes at 130°C or 266°F.

Forming .... Remove the bases, apply the bond to the back sides of the clay pieces, and bond two together.

Heating .... Cure in the oven for 40 minutes at 130°C or 266°F.

Finishing .... • Pierce a hole in the side of the clay pieces with a pin vise and string them on silver wire.
                                             • Attach the chains to the clay pieces with the wire at each side by winding it securely around the end of each chain (see Illustration A on p. 47).
                                             • Attach a clasp at the ends of the chains and fix with crimp beads.

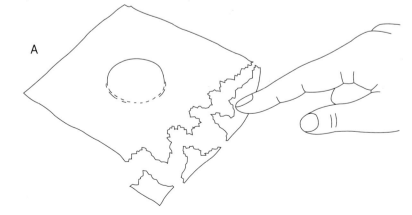

A

Materials

Polymer clay [premo!]

| Semitransparent: 1+3/4 segments of premo! 5310 (Translucent)

45 brass wires

| 5 for neck rings (total length of 2.45m or 8ft: each 490mm or 19.3in)

| 40 for clay piece frames (total length of 6.40m or 21ft: each 160mm or 6.3in)

1 clasp (spring ring and chain tab)

2 jump rings (small)

Sculpey® Bake & Bond

Preparation

Make frames for clay pieces with brass wire (40 pcs) (see Illustration below)

How to make

Conditioning ...... Use a polymer clay machine or dedicated pasta machine.

Forming .... • Pass the clay through the machine. Repeat, each time raising the setting on the dial, starting at No. 1 (2.6mm) to No. 8 (0.6mm) to gradually produce a thinner piece. Use parchment paper for No. 8 setting to prevent clay from tearing (see p. 38).

                              • Cut out a clay piece to the shape of the frame, apply the bond to the frame, and insert the clay.

Heating .... Heat in the oven for 40 minutes at 130°C or 266°F.

Finishing .... • Tie eight clay pieces to a neck ring in a good balance. Do the same to the other four neck rings.

                              • Put all five neck rings together while shifting the position of the clay pieces so that they layer nicely.

                              • Put the neck ring ends together, insert them through the jump ring, and wind securely. Attach a clasp to the jump ring (see Illustration A).

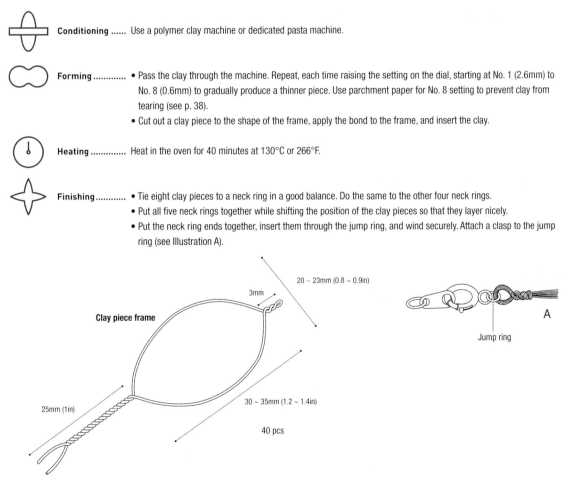

20 ~ 23mm (0.8 ~ 0.9in)

3mm

Clay piece frame

25mm (1in)

30 ~ 35mm (1.2 ~ 1.4in)

40 pcs

A

Jump ring

Materials

Polymer clay [FIMO CLASSIC and premo!]

Blue (front):	2+1/4 segments of premo! 5310 (Translucent), 1+3/5 segments of FIMO CLASSIC 34 (Navy Blue), small amount of FIMO CLASSIC 02 (Champagne) and 9 (Black)
Beige (back):	9 segments of FIMO CLASSIC 02 (Champagne), 1/3 segment of FIMO CLASSIC 0 (White), small amount of FIMO CLASSIC 77 (Chocolate) and 9 (Black)

54 eye pins

2 ribbons 3mm-wide (each 500mm or 19.7in long)

Sculpey® Bake & Bond

How to make

Conditioning ...... Use a polymer clay machine or dedicated pasta machine.

Color making ..... Make blue and beige.

Forming .... • Pass the beige clay through the machine at No. 1 (2.6mm).
- Pass the blue clay through the machine, each time raising the setting on the dial, starting at No. 1 (2.6mm) to No. 8 (0.6mm) to gradually produce a thinner piece. Use parchment paper for No. 8 setting to prevent the clay from tearing (see p. 38).
- Put the two clay sheets together by placing the blue clay with random pleats on the beige clay (see Illustration A)
- Cut out a total of 27 clay discs (6 large, 12 medium and 9 small), using clay cutters Ⓛ, Ⓜ and Ⓢ.
- Make holes on both sides and insert eye pins together with the bond.

Heating .... Cure in the oven for 40 minutes at 130°C or 266°F.

Finishing .... Join clay discs by connecting the eye pins and tie the ribbon at both ends.

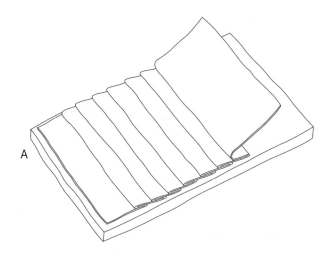

A

Materials

Polymer clay [premo!]

Bordeaux (front):	3 segments of FIMO CLASSIC 29 (Carmine), 1+1/2 segments of FIMO CLASSIC 23 (Bordeaux), small amount of FIMO CLASSIC 34 (Navy Blue) and 9 (Black)
White (front):	1/2 segment of FIMO CLASSIC 0 (White)
Black (back):	5+1/2 segments of FIMO CLASSIC 9 (Black)

23 silver wires

5 for bails (total length of 75mm or 3in: each 15mm)

18 for connectors (total length of 108mm or 4.3in: each 6mm)

1 nylon-coated wire (silver color, 580mm or 22.8in long)

1 clasp (spring ring and chain tab)

2 crimp beads

Sculpey® Bake & Bond

How to make

Conditioning ...... Use a polymer clay machine or dedicated pasta machine.

Color making ..... Make Bordeaux, and combine with white to create a marbled effect.

Forming .... • Pass clay through the machine at No. 2 (2.2mm).
- Cut out a total of 17 sets of Bordeaux and black clay discs (5 large, 5 medium and 7 small), using clay cutters Ⓛ, Ⓜ and Ⓢ.
- Combine the Bordeaux clay discs on top of the black ones. Make holes in the 13 clay discs, insert the silver wire together with the bond to connect them (see Illustration A). Affix four discs on top of these with the bond. Bend silver wire to make bails, apply the bond and fix to the back of the discs (see Illustration B).

Heating .... Cure in the oven for 40 minutes at 130°C or 266°F.

Finishing .... Put the nylon coated wire through the bails, attach a clasp at the end of it, and fix with crimp beads.

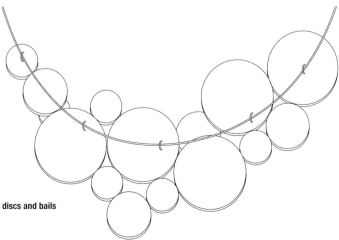

Positioning of discs and bails

Materials

Polymer clay [FIMO CLASSIC]

| Black: 4+1/2 segments of FIMO CLASSIC 9 (Black)

2 ball chains (total length of 1.26m or 4.1ft: 580mm or 22.8in and 680mm or 26.8in)

4 clamshell tips

1 clasp (spring ring and chain tab)

2 jump rings (small)

Sculpey® Bake & Bond

How to make

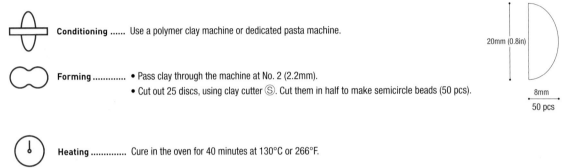

Conditioning ...... Use a polymer clay machine or dedicated pasta machine.

Forming .... • Pass clay through the machine at No. 2 (2.2mm).

• Cut out 25 discs, using clay cutter Ⓢ. Cut them in half to make semicircle beads (50 pcs).

20mm (0.8in)

8mm

50 pcs

Heating .... Cure in the oven for 40 minutes at 130°C or 266°F.

Forming .... Make a groove on the flat edges of each bead using a file, apply the bond to the grooves and attach them to the chain with even intervals (see Illustrations A and B).

Heating .... Reheat in the oven for 40 minutes at 130°C or 266°F.

Finishing .... Attach clamshell tips to the ends of the chain. Join two chain ends with jump rings and attach a clasp (see Illustration C).

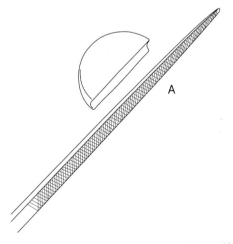

A

B

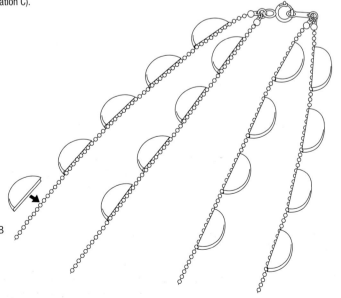

C

Materials

Polymer clay [FIMO CLASSIC]

Green (crescent beads): 6 segments of FIMO CLASSIC 5 (Green), 1+1/2 segments of FIMO CLASSIC 34 (Navy Blue)

Beige (spherical beads): 2+1/5 segments of FIMO CLASSIC 02 (Champagne), 1+4/5 segments of FIMO CLASSIC 0 (White), small amount of FIMO CLASSIC 17 (Ochre)

Semitransparent (spherical beads): 2+1/4 segments of premo! 5310 (Translucent)

White (spherical inner beads): 1/3 segment of FIMO CLASSIC 0 (White)

1 clasp (spring ring and chain tab)

2 jump rings (small)

22 jump rings (large)

Crescent beads

25mm (1in)   30mm (1.2in)

8mm
2 pcs

10mm
2 pcs

31mm (1.2in)   32mm (1.3in)   33mm (1.3in)   35mm (1.4in)

11mm
2 pcs

13mm
2 pcs

14mm
2 pcs

15mm
1 pcs

How to make

Crescent beads

Conditioning ...... Use a polymer clay machine or dedicated pasta machine.

Color making ..... Make green.

Forming .... • Pass clay through the machine at No. 1 (2.6mm).
• Cut out six discs, using clay cutter Ⓛ. Cut into a crescent shape and bevel corners (11 pcs).

Spherical beads

Conditioning ...... Use a polymer clay machine or dedicated pasta machine.

5mm
2 pcs

6mm
4 pcs

7mm
4 pcs

Spherical beads

Color making ..... Make beige.

Forming .... • Make balls with white clay to create inner beads (10 pcs).
• Pass the semitransparent and beige clays separately through the machine at No. 1 (2.6mm).
• Cut out four discs in each color, using clay cutter Ⓛ, and make wood-grain chips by referring to pages 38 and 39.
• Cover each inner bead with the wood-grain chips and roll to make it smooth.

Heating .... Cure in the oven for 40 minutes at 130°C or 266°F.

Finishing .... • Pierce each spherical bead with a pin vise, put an eye pin through, and make a loop at the end.
• Make holes at both ends of each crescent bead with a pin vise, and inset jump rings (large). Connect with spherical beads by joining the jump rings (large) and eye pin ends.
• Attach a clasp with jump rings (small).

Materials

Polymer clay [FIMO CLASSIC, FIMO EFFECT and premo!]

Color combination 1

Pearl:	1/6 segment of FIMO EFFECT 08 (Pearl)
Grey:	1/6 segment of FIMO EFFECT 08 (Pearl), small amount of FIMO CLASSIC 9 (Black)
Bordeaux:	1/6 segment of premo! 5310 (Translucent), small amount of FIMO CLASSIC 29 (Carmine), 23 (Bordeaux) and 9 (Black)
Yellow:	1/6 segment of premo! 5310 (Translucent), small amount of FIMO CLASSIC 1 (Yellow) and 15 (Golden Yellow)
Yellow-green:	1/6 segment of premo! 5310 (Translucent), small amount of FIMO CLASSIC 5 (Green) and a pinch of FIMO CLASSIC 34 (Navy Blue)

Color combination 2

Yellow:	1/6 segment of FIMO EFFECT 08 (Pearl), small amount of FIMO CLASSIC 1 (Yellow) and 15 (Golden Yellow)
Semitransparent:	1/6 segment of premo! 5310 (Translucent)
Blue:	1/6 segment of premo! 5310 (Translucent), small amount of FIMO CLASSIC 32 (Light Turquoise)
Blue-green:	1/6 segment of premo! 5310 (Translucent), small amount of FIMO CLASSIC 57 (Leaf Green) and 32 (Light Turquoise)
Green:	1/6 segment of premo! 5310 (Translucent), small amount of FIMO CLASSIC 57 (Leaf Green)

1 ball head pin

1 half-round ring (finished size: circumference approx. 53mm or 2in, fine silver clay: 3.5g or 0.1oz)

Metal adhesive

Preparation

Make a ring by referring to page 40. After drying, roughly polish with a sanding sponge pad, and make a hole. Make a groove (1mm deep and 3mm long) extending lengthwise from the hole. After firing, polish to give the inner surface a mirror finish and the outer surface a satin finish.

How to make

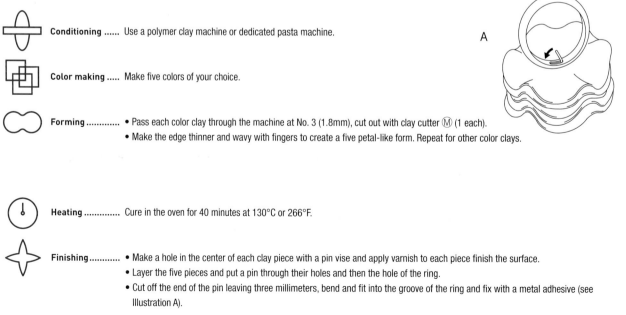

A

Conditioning ...... Use a polymer clay machine or dedicated pasta machine.

Color making ..... Make five colors of your choice.

Forming .... • Pass each color clay through the machine at No. 3 (1.8mm), cut out with clay cutter Ⓜ (1 each).

• Make the edge thinner and wavy with fingers to create a five petal-like form. Repeat for other color clays.

Heating .... Cure in the oven for 40 minutes at 130°C or 266°F.

Finishing .... • Make a hole in the center of each clay piece with a pin vise and apply varnish to each piece finish the surface.

• Layer the five pieces and put a pin through their holes and then the hole of the ring.

• Cut off the end of the pin leaving three millimeters, bend and fit into the groove of the ring and fix with a metal adhesive (see Illustration A).

Materials

Polymer clay [FIMO CLASSIC and premo!]

| Off-white: 1+3/4 segments of premo! 5310 (Translucent), 4 segments of FIMO CLASSIC 0 (White)

1 nylon-coated wire (gold color, 460mm or 18.1in long)

1 clasp (spring ring and chain tab)

2 crimp beads

Sculpey® Bake & Bond

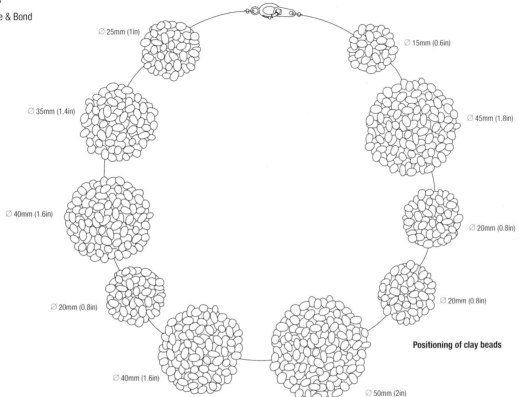

⌀ 25mm (1in)   ⌀ 15mm (0.6in)

⌀ 35mm (1.4in)   ⌀ 45mm (1.8in)

⌀ 40mm (1.6in)   ⌀ 20mm (0.8in)

⌀ 20mm (0.8in)   ⌀ 20mm (0.8in)

Positioning of clay beads

⌀ 40mm (1.6in)

⌀ 50mm (2in)

How to make

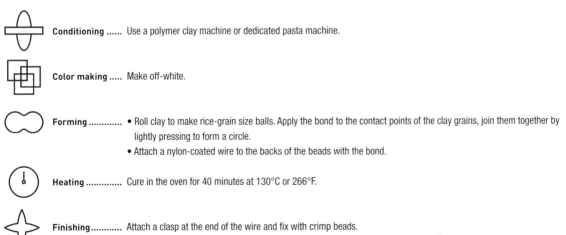

Conditioning ...... Use a polymer clay machine or dedicated pasta machine.

Color making ..... Make off-white.

Forming .... • Roll clay to make rice-grain size balls. Apply the bond to the contact points of the clay grains, join them together by lightly pressing to form a circle.
• Attach a nylon-coated wire to the backs of the beads with the bond.

Heating .... Cure in the oven for 40 minutes at 130°C or 266°F.

Finishing .... Attach a clasp at the end of the wire and fix with crimp beads.

Materials

Polymer clay [FIMO CLASSIC and premo!]

Dark brown:	1/4 segment of FIMO CLASSIC 77 (Chocolate), small amount of FIMO CLASSIC 23 (Bordeaux), 29 (Carmine) and 9 (Black)
Ochre:	2/5 segment of premo! 5310 (Translucent), small amount of FIMO CLASSIC 77 (Chocolate), 0 (White) and 9 (Black)
Beige:	2/5 segment of premo! 5310 (Translucent), small amount of FIMO CLASSIC 45 (Dark Flesh) and 17 (Ochre)
Semitransparent:	1/5 segment of premo! 5310 (Translucent)

1 necklace cord (430mm or 16.9in long)

6 beads (4 green and 2 brown)

1 toggle clasp

2 crimp beads

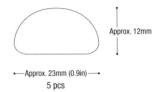

Approx. 12mm

— Approx. 23mm (0.9in) —

5 pcs

How to make

Conditioning ...... Use a polymer clay machine or dedicated pasta machine.

Color making ..... Make dark brown, ochre, and beige. Roughly combine them to create a marbled pattern.

Forming .... • Roll each color clay and make ropes (see Illustration A).
• Combine all clay ropes by hand until marbled and roll to make almond shape beads (5 pcs).

Heating .... Cure in the oven for 40 minutes at 130°C or 266°F.

Finishing .... • Pierce a hole in each with a pin vise bead and apply varnish to finish the surface of each bead.
• String all beads on the cord alternately, while securing each one by tying a knot at each end. Attach a toggle clasp at the end of the cord and fix with crimp beads.

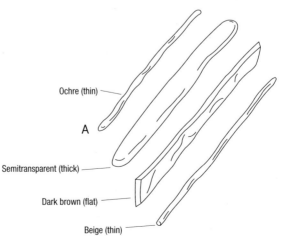

Ochre (thin)

A

Semitransparent (thick)

Dark brown (flat)

Beige (thin)

Materials

Polymer clay [FIMO CLASSIC]

| Black: | 2 segments of FIMO CLASSIC 9 (Black) |
| Semitransparent: | 2/5 segment of premo! 5310 (Translucent) |

27 flat rings (finished size: circumference approx. 55mm or 2.2in,

fine silver clay: 91.8g or 3.2oz)

13 ball head pins

2 jump rings (medium)

4 T-pins

2 ribbons 5mm-wide (each 1m or 3.3ft long)

Sphere sizes

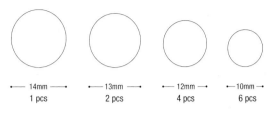

| ← 14mm → | ← 13mm → | ← 12mm → | ← 10mm → |
| 1 pcs | 2 pcs | 4 pcs | 6 pcs |

Preparation

- Make rings by referring to page 40. After drying, make a slit in each ring (see Illustration A). Join all rings by opening each one a little at the slit, rejoin the slit with clay paste to make chains A (13 rings), B (6 rings), C (5 rings), and D (3 rings).
- After firing, polish to give the inner surface a mirror finish and the outer surface a hammered finish.

How to make

Conditioning ...... Use a polymer clay machine or dedicated pasta machine.

Forming .... • Pass the black clay through the machine at No. 1 (2.6mm), and the semitransparent clay at No. 5 (1.2mm).
- Cut out eight sheets from each clay with clay cutter Ⓢ and layer alternately.
- Cut into pieces to make balls (13 spherical beads in small, medium and large sizes).

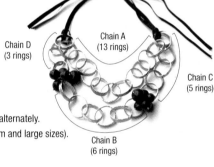

Chain D (3 rings)
Chain A (13 rings)
Chain C (5 rings)
Chain B (6 rings)

Heating .... Cure in the oven for 40 minutes at 130°C or 266°F.

Finishing .... • To join chains B and C, and B and D, make holes in the end rings, put a T-pin through from the inside of each ring, make a loop outside, and join the loops with jump rings (see Illustration B).
- Pierce each clay bead with a pin vise and apply varnish to finish the surface. By putting a ball head pin through each bead, attach all clay beads to the jump rings between chains B and C, and B and D (see Illustration B).
- Put the end rings of chains A and C, and A and D together, and pass ribbons through as shown above.

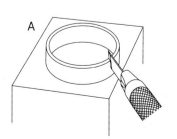

A

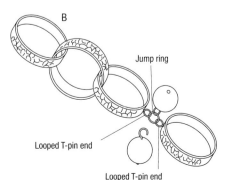

B

Jump ring

Looped T-pin end

Looped T-pin end

Materials

Polymer clay [FIMO CLASSIC and premo!]

Light blue (flower center):	Small amount of premo! 5310 (Translucent), FIMO CLASSIC 32 (Light Turquoise) and 57 (Leaf Green)
Black (flower):	1 segment of FIMO CLASSIC 9 (Black)
Semitransparent (flower):	1/4 segment of premo! 5310 (Translucent)
Black (sphere beads):	Small amount of FIMO CLASSIC 9 (Black)

8 flat rings (finished size: circumference approx. 55mm or 2.2in, fine silver clay: 27.2g or 1oz)

1 ball chain (40mm or 1.6in long)

2 clamshell tips

1 clasp (spring ring and chain tab)

2 jump rings (small)

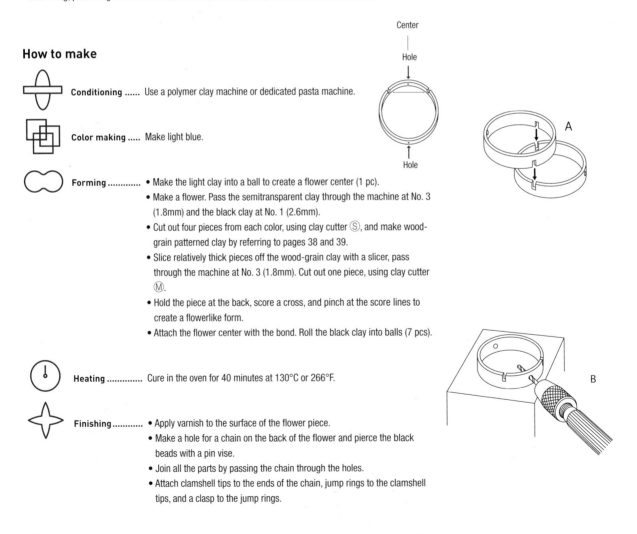

Flower

Flower center

Spherical beads

4mm — 7 pcs   7.5mm — 1 pc   25mm (1in) — 1 pc

Preparation

• Make rings by referring to page 40. After drying, make slits in each ring so that two can be combined (see Illustration A). Make holes for the chain (see Illustration B).

• After firing, polish to give the inner surface a mirror finish and the outer surface a satin finish.

How to make

Center

Hole

A

Hole

B

Conditioning ...... Use a polymer clay machine or dedicated pasta machine.

Color making ..... Make light blue.

Forming .... • Make the light clay into a ball to create a flower center (1 pc).
- Make a flower. Pass the semitransparent clay through the machine at No. 3 (1.8mm) and the black clay at No. 1 (2.6mm).
- Cut out four pieces from each color, using clay cutter Ⓢ, and make wood-grain patterned clay by referring to pages 38 and 39.
- Slice relatively thick pieces off the wood-grain clay with a slicer, pass through the machine at No. 3 (1.8mm). Cut out one piece, using clay cutter Ⓜ.
- Hold the piece at the back, score a cross, and pinch at the score lines to create a flowerlike form.
- Attach the flower center with the bond. Roll the black clay into balls (7 pcs).

Heating .... Cure in the oven for 40 minutes at 130°C or 266°F.

Finishing .... • Apply varnish to the surface of the flower piece.
- Make a hole for a chain on the back of the flower and pierce the black beads with a pin vise.
- Join all the parts by passing the chain through the holes.
- Attach clamshell tips to the ends of the chain, jump rings to the clamshell tips, and a clasp to the jump rings.

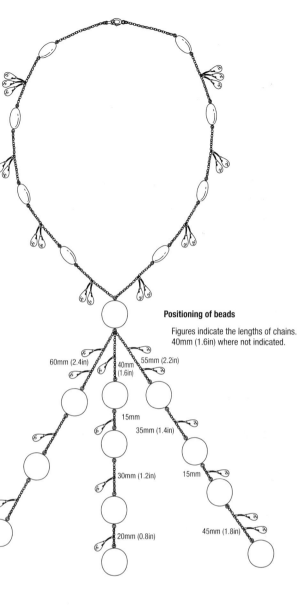

Materials

Polymer clay [FIMO CLASSIC and premo!]

Dark green:	1+1/4 segments of premo! 5310 (Translucent), small amount of FIMO CLASSIC 34 (Navy Blue) and 57 (Leaf Green)
Green:	3+4/5 segments of premo! 5310 (Translucent), and small amount of FIMO CLASSIC 57 (Leaf Green) and 34 (Navy Blue)

32 droplet beads

3 ball head pins

17 eye pins

21 chains (total of 795mm or 31.3in: cut into given lengths)

1 silver wire (640mm or 25.2in long)

1 clasp (spring ring and chain tab)

2 jump rings (small)

Positioning of beads

Figures indicate the lengths of chains.
40mm (1.6in) where not indicated.

60mm (2.4in)   40mm (1.6in)   55mm (2.2in)

15mm   35mm (1.4in)   30mm (1.2in)   15mm   20mm (0.8in)   45mm (1.8in)

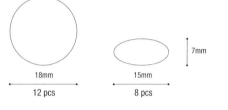

18mm — 12 pcs

7mm

15mm — 8 pcs

How to make

Conditioning ...... Use a polymer clay machine or dedicated pasta machine.

Color making ..... Make dark green and green.

Forming .... • Roll each piece of clay into a cylinder.
• Grate two color cylinders together with a grater. Put the grated pieces together firmly and make designated sizes and shapes (12 spherical beads and 8 oval beads).

Heating .... Cure in the oven for 40 minutes at 130°C or 266°F.

Finishing .... • Polish the clay beads first with a sanding sponge pad, then with a buffer, and pierce holes with a pin vise.
• Put ball head pins through the three end beads and eye pins through the rest.
• Connect the beads with chains while bending the ends of the pins into a loop.
• Put together the ends of the silver wires which join the droplets to the chains, and fix them securely by winding them a few times (see Illustration A).
• Attach a clasp to the ends of chains with jump rings.

A

Materials

Polymer clay [FIMO CLASSIC, FIMO EFFECT and premo!]

Ivory:	1+3/4 segments of premo! 5310 (Translucent), 1/3 segment of FIMO CLASSIC 02 (Champagne), small amount of FIMO CLASSIC 17 (Ochre)
Gold:	Small amount of FIMO EFFECT 11 (Metal Gold)

8 flat rings (finished size: circumference approx. 55mm or 2.2in, fine silver clay: 27.2g or 1oz)

1 nylon-coated wire (gold color, 490mm or 19.3in long)

145 metal color beads

70 eye pins

1 clasp (spring ring and chain tab)

2 crimp beads

Sculpey® Bake & Bond

How to make

Conditioning ...... Use a polymer clay machine or dedicated pasta machine.

Color making ..... Make ivory.

Forming .... • Take a small amount of clay and make a ball with fingers, roll it up and down to create a needle form. Repeat this and make a total of seventy short and long needles.
• Add a small amount of metallic gold clay to the narrower end of some of these needles for contrast and make the surface smooth.
• Apply the bond to an eye pin and insert it into the thicker end of each clay needle (see Illustration below). Twist some to create movement.

Heating .... Cure in the oven for 40 minutes at 130°C or 266°F.

Finishing .... • String metal color beads onto a nylon-coated wire to a length of 160mm or 6.3in, and then alternate using all the clay needles, and finish with metal color beads for another 160mm or 6.3in.
• Attach a clasp to the ends of the wire with crimp beads.

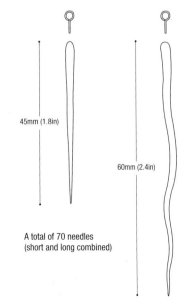

45mm (1.8in)

60mm (2.4in)

A total of 70 needles
(short and long combined)

Materials

Polymer clay [FIMO CLASSIC and premo!]

Dark Brown:	4/5 segment of FIMO CLASSIC 77 (Chocolate), small amount of premo! 5310 (Translucent) and FIMO CLASSIC 9 (Black)
Brown:	3/5 segment of FIMO CLASSIC 77 (Chocolate), small amount of FIMO CLASSIC 23 (Bordeaux), 29 (Carmine), premo! 5310 (Translucent) and FIMO CLASSIC 9 (Black)
Reddish brown:	2/5 segment of FIMO CLASSIC 77 (Chocolate), small amount of premo! 5310 (Translucent), FIMO CLASSIC 23 (Bordeaux), 29 (Carmine) and 02 (Champagne)
Caramel:	1/4 segment of premo! 5310 (Translucent), small amount of FIMO CLASSIC 17 (Ochre) and 77 (Chocolate)
Semitransparent:	1/4 segment of premo! 5310 (Translucent)

45 nylon wires

3 for neck ring (total length of 1.29m or 4.2ft: each 430mm or 16.9in)

42 for hanging strands (total length of 9,66m or 31.7ft: 6 each of the 7 lengths)

1 clasp (spring ring and chain tab)

2 crimp beads

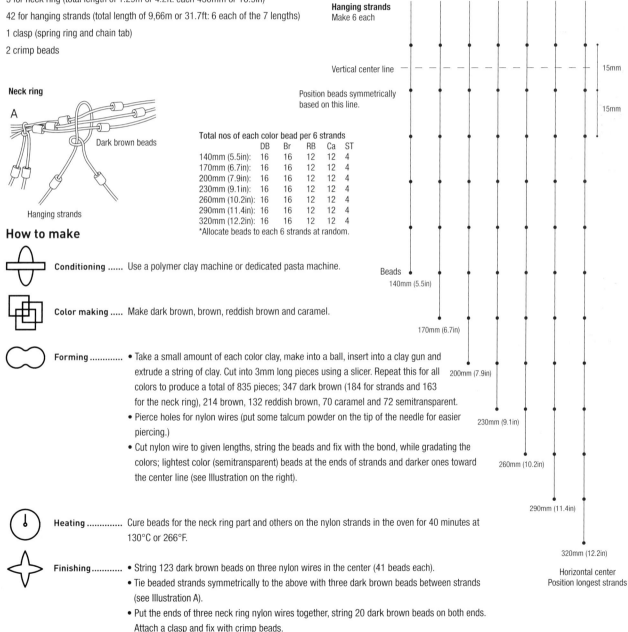

Hanging strands
Make 6 each

Vertical center line

Position beads symmetrically based on this line.

Neck ring

A

Dark brown beads

Hanging strands

Total nos of each color bead per 6 strands

	DB	Br	RB	Ca	ST
140mm (5.5in):	16	16	12	12	4
170mm (6.7in):	16	16	12	12	4
200mm (7.9in):	16	16	12	12	4
230mm (9.1in):	16	16	12	12	4
260mm (10.2in):	16	16	12	12	4
290mm (11.4in):	16	16	12	12	4
320mm (12.2in):	16	16	12	12	4

*Allocate beads to each 6 strands at random.

15mm

15mm

Beads
140mm (5.5in)

170mm (6.7in)

200mm (7.9in)

230mm (9.1in)

260mm (10.2in)

290mm (11.4in)

320mm (12.2in)

Horizontal center
Position longest strands

How to make

Conditioning ...... Use a polymer clay machine or dedicated pasta machine.

Color making ..... Make dark brown, brown, reddish brown and caramel.

Forming .... • Take a small amount of each color clay, make into a ball, insert into a clay gun and extrude a string of clay. Cut into 3mm long pieces using a slicer. Repeat this for all colors to produce a total of 835 pieces; 347 dark brown (184 for strands and 163 for the neck ring), 214 brown, 132 reddish brown, 70 caramel and 72 semitransparent.
• Pierce holes for nylon wires (put some talcum powder on the tip of the needle for easier piercing.)
• Cut nylon wire to given lengths, string the beads and fix with the bond, while gradating the colors; lightest color (semitransparent) beads at the ends of strands and darker ones toward the center line (see Illustration on the right).

Heating .... Cure beads for the neck ring part and others on the nylon strands in the oven for 40 minutes at 130°C or 266°F.

Finishing .... • String 123 dark brown beads on three nylon wires in the center (41 beads each).
• Tie beaded strands symmetrically to the above with three dark brown beads between strands (see Illustration A).
• Put the ends of three neck ring nylon wires together, string 20 dark brown beads on both ends. Attach a clasp and fix with crimp beads.

Materials

Polymer clay [FIMO CLASSIC and premo!]

Semitransparent:	3/5 segment of premo! 5310 (Translucent)
Black:	2/3 segment of FIMO CLASSIC 9 (Black)

1 nylon-coated wire (silver color, 440mm or 12.2in long)

1 clasp (spring ring and chain tab)

2 crimp beads

How to make

Conditioning ...... Use a polymer clay machine or dedicated pasta machine.

Forming .... • Roll clay and make a ball with fingers, roll it up and down to create a rope form.
• Cut into given lengths. Join two different color ropes by rolling with fingers (see Illustration A).
• Make both ends pointy (62 pcs).

Heating .... Cure in the oven for 40 minutes at 130°C or 266°F.

Finishing .... Pierce each bead near the end with a pin vise, string beads on nylon-coated wire and attach a clasp at the end of the wire and fix with crimp beads.

Choker

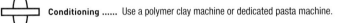

2mm   ⟷ _____ _____ Semitransparent
        ←—— 15mm ——→

2mm   ⟷ _____ _____ Black
        ←—10mm—→

_____ A

←———— 30mm (1.2in) ————→   62 pcs

←—— 4mm

Materials

Polymer clay [FIMO CLASSIC and premo!]

Semitransparent:	Small amount of premo! 5310 (Translucent)
Black:	Small amount of FIMO CLASSIC 9 (Black)

1 set of pierced earring findings

1 silver wire (300mm or 11.8in long)

Sculpey® Bake & Bond

How to make

- Make 10 beads in the same way as for the choker (p. 60)
- Cure in the oven for 40 minutes at 130°C or 266°F.
- Put silver wire through the hole, wind two to three times to fix, and attach to an earring finding (see Illustration B).

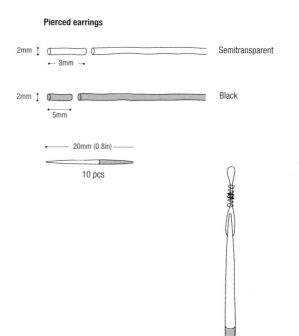

Pierced earrings

2mm — ← 8mm → — Semitransparent

2mm — 5mm — Black

← 20mm (0.8in) →

10 pcs

B

Materials

Polymer clay [FIMO CLASSIC and premo!]

Semitransparent:	1/4 segment of premo! 5310 (Translucent)
Black:	Small amount of FIMO CLASSIC 9 (Black)

1 eye pin

1 jump ring

1 chain (450mm or 17.7in long)

1 clasp (spring ring and chain tab)

2 jump rings (small)

Sculpey® Bake & Bond

How to make

- Make 70 clay pieces in the same way as for the pierced earrings above.
- Cure in the oven for 40 minutes at 130°C or 266°F.
- Make a half-sphere base with semitransparent clay, insert an eye pin with the bond. Insert the clay pieces in a good balance (see Illustration C).
- Cure again in the oven for 40 minutes at 130°C or 266°F.
- Put a chain through the eye pin and attach a clasp with jump rings.

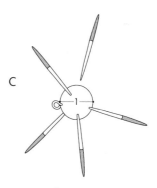

C

10mm Φ (size of the half-sphere base)

Materials

Polymer clay [premo!]

| Semitransparent: 1/5 segment of premo! 5310 (Translucent)

14 ball head pins

4 brass wires

| 2 for clay pieces (total length of 100mm or 3.9in: 50mm or 2in each)

| 2 for earring findings (total length of 100mm or 3.9in: 50mm or 2in each)

Sculpey® Bake & Bond

How to make

Conditioning ...... Use a polymer clay machine or dedicated pasta machine.

Forming .... • Make a ball with clay, insert into the clay gun, and extrude a string. Cut into given lengths (14 pieces).
                         • Insert a ball head pin with the bond at the tip of each clay piece (Illustration A-1). Bundle seven pieces together at the ends.

Heating .... Cure in the oven for 40 minutes at 130°C or 266°F.

Finishing .... • Bind the bundled ends with brass wire and bend the end of the wire into a loop (see Illustration A-2).
                         • Bend the brass wire to make earring findings and attach to the clay pieces (see Illustration A-3).

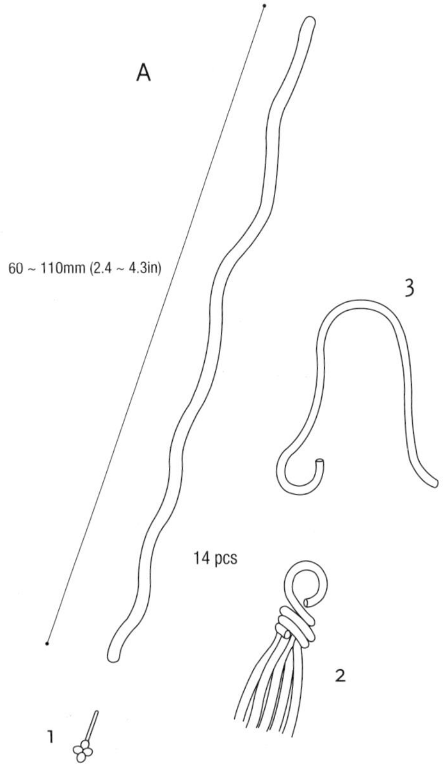

A

60 ~ 110mm (2.4 ~ 4.3in)

3

14 pcs

2

1

Materials

Polymer clay [FIMO CLASSIC, FIMO EFFECT and premo!]

Wine (petals):	1+2/5 segments of FIMO CLASSIC 23 (Bordeaux), small amount of FIMO CLASSIC 9 (Black), 29 (Carmine), and FIMO EFFECT 08 (Pearl)
Black (base):	1/3 segment of FIMO CLASSIC 9 (Black)

1 flat ring (finished size: circumference approx. 55mm or 2.2in, fine silver clay: 3.4g)

130 brass wires (total of 1.3m or 4.3ft long: each 10mm long)

1 chain (480mm or 18.9in long)

1 jump ring (medium)

1 key eye (fine silver)

Sculpey® Bake & Bond

Preparation

• Make a ring by referring to page 40. After drying, make a hammered pattern using a half-round file (see Illustration A).
  Make a hole, insert a key eye, and apply paste-type silver clay on the end.

• After firing, polish to give the surface a satin finish.

How to make

Conditioning ...... Use a polymer clay machine or dedicated pasta machine.

Color making ..... Make wine color.

Forming .... • Take a small amount of clay, make a tear drop and squash into a petal form with fingers (120 pcs).
• Apply the bond to brass wires and insert in the bases of the petals (see Illustration B).

Heating .... Cure in the oven for 40 minutes at 130°C or 266°F.

Forming .... • Fill the ring with black clay in a mound to make the base.
• Apply the bond to the brass wire of the petals and insert in the base (see Illustration B).

Heating .... Cure in the oven for 40 minutes at 130°C or 266°F.

Finishing .... Attach a jump ring to the key eye and put a chain through it.

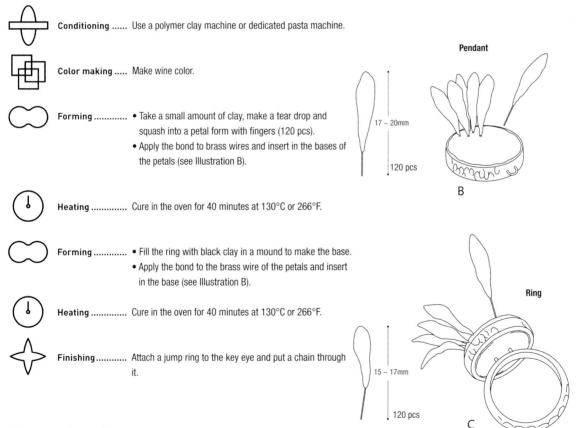

How to make a ring

• Make the top part of the ring in the same way as the pendant above.

• Make a half-round ring with a hammered pattern. Finish by referring to the instructions for the ring No. 26 (p. 65), and attach to the top part by inserting it into the back of the clay base (see Illustration C).

Materials

Polymer clay [FIMO CLASSIC and premo!]

Pink:	4 segments of premo! 5310 (Translucent), small amount of FIMO CLASSIC 2 (Red),
Ochre:	1 segment of FIMO CLASSIC 0 (White), small amount of 77 (Chocolate) and 9 (Black)
Inner beads:	3+2/5 segments of premo! 5310 (Translucent), 1 segment of FIMO CLASSIC 0 (White), small amount of FIMO CLASSIC 2 (Red) and 77 (Chocolate)

31 eye pins

9 jump rings

1 chain (375mm or 14.8in, cut to given lengths)

Sculpey® Bake & Bond

How to make

Conditioning ...... Use a polymer clay machine or dedicated pasta machine.

Color making ..... Make pink and ochre.

Forming .... • Pass each color clay through the machine at No. 1 (2.6mm). Cut out seven pink sheets and one ochre sheet using clay cutter Ⓛ. Layer these sheets, cut in half, and layer again. Make wood-grain chips by referring to pages 38 and 39.
• Combine all clays for the inner beads to make into spheres (total of 31 small, medium and large).
• Cover the entire surface of the inner beads with the chips, and roll until smooth.
• Make holes in the medium and small beads and insert eye pins with the bond.

Heating .... Cure in the oven for 40 minutes at 130°C or 266°F.

Finishing .... • Polish the beads with a sanding sponge pad first and then with a buffer. Pierce the large beads with a pin vise, insert eye pins into the large beads and bend the ends into loops (see Illustration A). Join with chains.
• Attach small- and medium-size beads with jump rings to the chains.

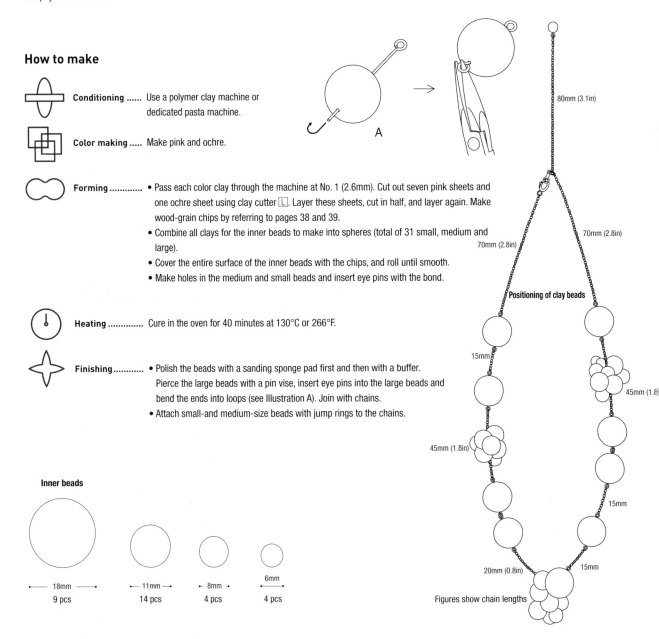

A

80mm (3.1in)

70mm (2.8in)

70mm (2.8in)

Positioning of clay beads

15mm

45mm (1.8in)

45mm (1.8in)

15mm

15mm

20mm (0.8in)

15mm

Figures show chain lengths

Inner beads

18mm	11mm	8mm	6mm
9 pcs	14 pcs	4 pcs	4 pcs

Materials (for 1 ring)

Polymer clay [FIMO CLASSIC, FIMO EFFECT and premo!]

Off-white (background):	4 segments of FIMO CLASSIC 0 (White), small amount of FIMO CLASSIC 57 (Leaf Green) and 9 (Black)
Semitransparent (background):	2+1/4 segments of premo! 5310 (Translucent)
White (patterns):	Small amount of FIMO CLASSIC 0 (White)
Black (patterns):	Small amount of FIMO CLASSIC 9 (Black)
Bordeaux (base):	1/2 segment of FIMO CLASSIC 23 (Bordeaux), small amount of FIMO CLASSIC 29 (Carmine)
Black (base):	Small amount of FIMO CLASSIC 9 (Black)

2 rings (ring top frame: flat ring with finished size: circumference approx. 55mm or 2.2in/ring: half-round ring with finished size: circumference approx. 53mm or 2in, fine silver clay: 6.9g or 0.2oz)

2 fine silver wires (total of 10mm: each 5mm long)

Sculpey® Bake & Bond

Preparation

• Make rings by referring to page 40. After drying, make two holes on the side of the ring, and apply paste-type silver clay to the fine silver wires and insert them into the holes.

• After firing, polish the side of the top frame to give it a satin finish and the top edge a mirror finish, while polishing the outer surface of the ring to give it a satin finish and the inner surface a mirror finish.

How to make

Conditioning ...... Use a polymer clay machine or dedicated pasta machine.

Color making ..... Make off-white and Bordeaux.

B

C

Forming ....
- Pass the off-white and semitransparent clays through the machine at No. 1 (2.6mm).
- Cut out four pieces in each color, using clay cutter Ⓛ, and make wood-grain patterned chips by referring to pages 38 and 39.
- Pass the Bordeaux clay for the base through the machine at No. 1 (2.6mm), cover with the chips, and cut out using clay cutter Ⓜ to make a disc.
- Make the clay for patterns into strings or spheres, place on the clay disc to create patterns (see Illustration A), and pass through the machine at No. 1 (2.6mm).
- Pass the black clay for the base through the machine at No. 3 (1.8mm), place the patterned clay above on it and cut out using clay cutter Ⓢ.
- Apply the bond to the side of the clay disc and fit in the top frame (see Illustration B).
- Apply the bond to the fine silver wires of the ring and insert in the back of the top disc (see Illustration C).

Heating .... Cure in the oven for 40 minutes at 130°C or 266°F.

A

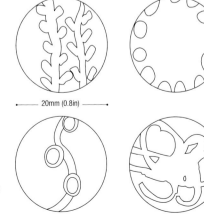

20mm (0.8in)

Pattern examples

Inner bead

← 14mm →

16 pcs

Materials

Polymer clay [FIMO CLASSIC, FIMO EFFECT and premo!]

Pink:	3/5 segment of premo! 5310 (Translucent), small amount of FIMO CLASSIC 2 (Red)
Green:	3/5 segment of premo! 5310 (Translucent), small amount of FIMO CLASSIC 5 (Green)
Ochre:	3/5 segment of premo! 5310 (Translucent), small amount of FIMO CLASSIC 15 (Golden Yellow) and 2 (Red)
Semitransparent:	1+1/5 segments of premo! 5310 (Translucent)
Pearl:	1+1/2 segments of FIMO EFFECT 08 (Pearl)
Black:	4/5 segment of FIMO EFFECT 9 (Black)
Chocolate:	Small amount of FIMO EFFECT 77 (Chocolate)

15 pcs gold leaf (each 40mm or 1.6in square)

1 nylon-coated wire (gold color: 280mm or 11in long)

2 jump rings

2 crimp beads

34 ribbons 3mm-wide (4 x 250mm or 9.8in long, 30 x 60mm or 2.4in long)

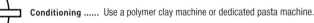

A

B

How to make

Conditioning ...... Use a polymer clay machine or dedicated pasta machine.

Color making ..... Make pink, green and ochre.

Forming .... • Pass each of the three mixed color clays through the machine at No. 1 (2.6mm), and cut out one sheet each using clay cutter ⬜.
- Combine a sheet of semitransparent clay with each color sheet above, and pass through the machine separately at No. 1 (2.6mm), repeat until achieving a nice gradation, and pass through the machine at No. 3 (1.8mm) to finish.
- Pass the black and pearl clays separately through the machine at No. 3 (1.8mm).
- Cut out three sheets each of all five clays using clay cutter ⬜.
- Layer a gold leaf and each sheet of the five clays alternately to make three blocks, and make wood-grain chips with gold leaf by referring to page 39.
- Combine the remaining clay with chocolate color clay, roll and make inner beads (16 pcs). Cover the entire surface of these with the chips above, and roll until smooth.

Heating .... Cure in the oven for 40 minutes at 130°C or 266°F.

Finishing .... • Polish the beads first with a sanding sponge pad and then with a buffer.
- Pierce the beads and string with nylon-coated wire. Bend the end of the wire into a loop, attach ribbons bundled with a crimp bead with a jump ring (see Illustration A-1)
- Tie shorter ribbons between the beads (see Illustration A-2).

Inner bead

— 10mm →

6 pcs

Materials (for 1 ring)

Polymer clay [FIMO EFFECT and Sculpey III]

| Semitransparent: | Small amount of Sulpey III 010 (Translucent) |
| Pearl: | 2/3 segment of FIMO EFFECT 08 (Pearl) |

6 flat rings (finished size: circumference approx. 55mm or 2.2in, fine silver clay: 21g)

7 glass beads (small)

7 eye pins

6 fine silver wires (total length of 114mm or 4.5in: each 19mm)

1 clasp (spring ring and chain tab)

12 key eyes (fine silver)

Metal adhesive

Preparation

• Make a ring by referring to page 40. After drying, roughly polish with a sanding sponge pad, and make two indents on the inner side of the ring (see Illustration A).

• Make two holes on the outer side, and insert key eyes, applying paste-type silver clay on their ends.

• After firing, polish to give the inner surface a mirror finish and the outer surface a satin finish.

How to make

Conditioning ...... Condition only the pearl clay, using a polymer clay machine or dedicated pasta machine.

Forming .... • Referring to page 39, transfer a design of your choice to the semitransparent clay.
• Cover the inner bead with the above clay with the printed side down.
• Cut excess clay (see Illustration B) away and roll until smooth.

Heating .... Cure in the oven for 40 minutes at 130°C or 266°F.

Finishing .... • Make a hole in the center of each clay piece and apply varnish to finish the surface.
• Pierce the bead and insert a silver wire, apply metal adhesive to the ends of the wire and fit them in the indents inside the ring (see Illustration C).
• Join the rings and glass beads with eye pins. Attach a clasp to the end eye pins.

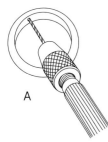

A

B

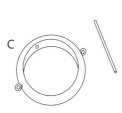

C

Materials (for 1 ring)

Polymer clay [FIMO CLASSIC, FIMO EFFECT, Sculpey III and premo!]

Semitransparent:	Small amount of Sulpey III 010 (Translucent)
Pearl (base):	1/2 segment of FIMO EFFECT 08 (Pearl)
Ochre (base):	1/4 segment of premo! 5310 (Translucent), small amount of FIMO CLASSIC 77 (Chocolate), 0 (White), and 9 (Black)

1 flat ring (finished size: circumference approx. 48mm or 1.9in, fine silver clay: 2.9g or 0.1oz)

1 bead necklace (3 strands, 400mm or 15.7in long)

1 pc thick paper (40mm x 120mm or 1.6in x 4.7in)

Sculpey Bake & Bond

Preparation

- Roll a thick piece of paper to make an oval cylinder base (see Illustration A).
- Make a ring by referring to page 40. After drying, cut out a six millimeter wide opening to match the thickness of the pendant. Do not make it too large.
- After firing, polish to give the inner and side surfaces a mirror finish and the outer surface a satin finish. Squash the ring with fingers to make an oval bail.

How to make

Conditioning ...... Use a polymer clay machine or dedicated pasta machine.

Color making ..... Make ochre.

Forming ....
- Referring to page 39, transfer a design of your choice to the semitransparent clay.
- Pass the pearl and ochre clays through the machine at No. 2 (2.2mm) two or three times.
- Place the semitransparent clay on the pearl clay with the printed side down, so that the print does not rub off. Layer this on the ochre clay, and cut into a 27mm by 42mm or 1.1in by 1.7in piece.
- Cut out a small opening (4mm by 1.5mm) for the bail attachment. Place on the paper cylinder base to form a curve (see Illustration A).

Heating .... Cure in the oven for 40 minutes at 130°C or 266°F.

Forming .... Apply the bond to the opening of the clay pendant and attach the bail.

Heating .... Cure in the oven for 40 minutes at 130°C or 266°F.

Finishing ....
- Apply varnish to finish the surface.
- Insert the bead necklace through the bail.

A

Accessories: names and uses

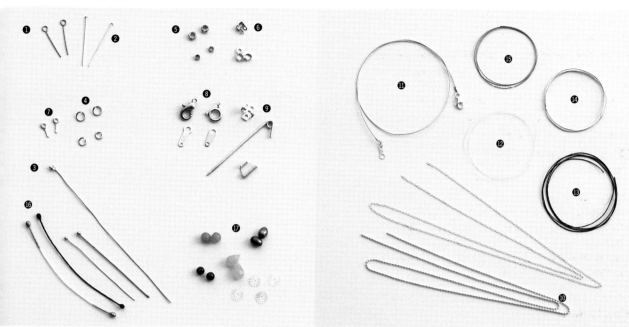

❶ Eye pin
A pin with looped head. By looping the other end also, you can join a bead or the like on both its ends.

❷ T-pin
A head pin with a T-form head. You cannot join anything to the head. Loop the other end for this purpose.

❸ Ball head pin
A head pin with a ball form head. Can be used in the same way as T-pins, but is usually longer with more applications.

❹ Jump ring
A circular metal ring used as a connector between an eye pin or T-pin and a bead or chain.

❺ Crimp bead
A stopper bead to fix a wire or cord. Use by stringing the wire.

❻ Clamshell tip
A connector with a connecting hook, used at the ends of a ball chain.

❼ Key eye (fine silver)
Designed specially for fine silver clay. Used by inserting the end into clay. Oven safe.

❽ Spring ring/Chain tab
A clasp for necklaces and other pieces of jewelry, consisting of an openable spring ring and tab with a hole.

❾ Brooch pin
A brooch fastener consisting of a spring needle and catch.

❿ Chain
A cable chain (above) and ball chain (below).

⓫ Neck wire
A necklace wire with a clasp. Ready to use as is.

⓬ Nylon wire
Nylon fishing wire. Easy to use for necklaces, because of its transparency and firmness.

⓭ Beading thread
It comes in diverse materials, including cotton and linen, and is stronger than sewing thread.

⓮ Silver wire
Used for connecting clay beads or other parts. Those of fine silver wire are oven safe. Suitable for making a wrapped loop.

⓯ Brass wire (Color wire)
An alloy of copper and zinc. Make good use of the color gold.

⓰ Artificial stamen
An element for artificial flowers. Used for the center of the clay flower in this book.

⓱ Beads
Available in various materials, forms, and sizes. Select based on your design.

How to attach a spring ring and chain tab

Using a jump ring (left)
Open in a twisting motion using pliers, insert a spring ring (or chain tab) and close.

Using a crimp bead (right)
String a crimp bead and spring ring (or chain tab) on a wire, put the wire back through the crimp bead, and squeeze with pliers.

Tools

Some can be substituted with tools you already have. Purchase one by one as needed.

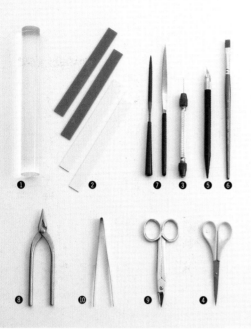

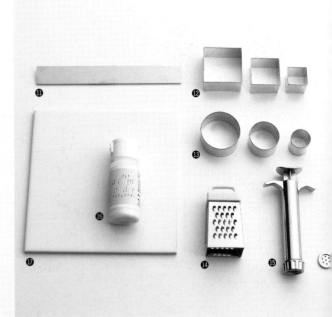

Conditioning/Forming

❶ Rolling pin

A cylindrical tool to flatten clay (substitutable with one for pastry, but do not use for both purposes).

❷ Thickness gauge strips

Used to gauge thickness (0.5mm ~ 2.0mm) when rolling clay (substitutable with playing cards or the like).

❸ Pin vise

Small drill with a blade (0.8mm, 1.0mm or 1.3mm) used for making holes (usable for both polymer and silver clays).

❹ Teflon scissors for polymer clay

Nonstick scissors with thin Teflon blades for fine clay work.

❺ Cutter

Used to cut clay into desired shapes.

❻ Art brush

Used when applying gold leaf or transferring photocopied patterns.

❼ Half-round medium-grit file

Used for polishing and finishing clay after firing (usable for both polymer and silver clays).

❽ Pliers

Used for assembling metal parts.

❾ Crown scissors

Used to cut silver wire or other metal parts (substitutable with nippers or all-purpose scissors).

❿ Tweezers

Used to hold silver clay after firing.

⓫ Slicer

Used to divide and cut clay. Its thin and supple blade enables the cutting of curves (substitutable with a cutter blade).

⓬ Clay cutter (square)

Used to cut out clay. Comes in three sizes: large (40mm or 1.6in sq), medium (30mm or 1.2in sq) and small (20mm or 0.8in sq).

⓭ Clay cutter (round)

Used to cut out clay. Comes in three sizes; large (40mm or 1.6in Φ), medium (30mm or 1.2in Φ) and small (20mm or 0.8in Φ).

⓮ Grater

Used to make clay into small pieces (substitutable with a cheese grater, but do not use for both purposes).

⓯ Clay gun

Used to extrude clay into a thin cord. The thickness of the cord is adjustable with a disc attached at the end.

⓰ Talcum powder

Used to thinly powder the clay surface or mold for easy mold release (substitutable with baby powder).

⓱ Tile

Used to work clay on and can be heated together with clay.

Polishing

⑱ Rubber block

A stand for polishing.

⑲ Varnish

Gives a luster to polymer clay after curing.

⑳ Sanding sponge pad

A sheet of sponge with abrasive. Used wet to polish polymer clay after curing. Good for curved surfaces (usable for both clay and silver clay).

㉑ Waterproof sandpaper

Used for wet polishing of polymer clay after heating. Good for flat surfaces and details (usable for both clay and silver clay).

㉒ Rotary tool

An electric tool used at the finishing stage to polish or give luster to clay and silver clay.

㉓ Cloth buff

A cloth buff rotary tool attachment used for final buffing of polymer clay after curing and wet polishing (substitutable with flannel when wet polishing with a 1200 or coarser grit sandpaper).

㉔ Bristle discs

A radial-shaped rotary tool attachment used to polish silver clay. Obtain desired mirror finish by adjusting grit level from coarse to fine by changing the color of the disc.

㉕ Silver polishing cloth

Cloth with abrasive, used for final polishing of silver clay.

㉖ Wenol

Silver polish used for final polishing of silver clay. Apply using a silver polishing cloth.

㉗ Fine tipped burnisher (ultra-hard)

A burnisher with a hard tip. Used to polish the surface of silver clay by pressing motion to obtain a mirror finish.

㉘ Stainless steel brush

Used to remove white crystalline powder from the surface of silver clay to reveal the silver surface immediately after firing. (Substitutable with a sanding sponge or waterproof sandpaper.)

Others

㉙ Perfect Gel

An acrylic emulsion-type all-purpose adhesive for clay, metal, cloth, wood, leather, and various other materials. Sculpey Bake & Bond is known for its use with polymer clays which bond when fired.

㉚ Lubricant oil

Used as a release agent for silver clay (substitutable with olive oil).

㉛ Core material (woodchip clay)

Used as an inner material when making a large piece.

㉜ Silver roller

Used to remove air from silver clay at the beginning of forming, or to roll into a cord (substitutable with a CD case).

㉝ Jeweler's hammer

A small-size hammer, used to create a hammered finish surface on silver clay.

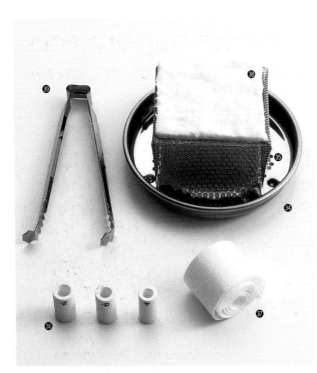

Suppliers

Polymer clay:
FIMO CLASSIC/FIMO EFFECT
STAEDTLER Mars GmbH & Co. KG.
http://www.staedtler.com

premo! Sulpey/Sulpey III
Polyform Products Company
http://www.sculpey.com

Fine silver clay:
PMC3 (Precious Metal Clay)
Mitsubishi Materials Corporation
http://www.mmc.co.jp/pmc/english/index.html
Distributors/Agencies
http://www.mmc.co.jp/pmc/english/distributors.html

Art Clay Silver 650 (Art Clay Silver)
Aida Chemical Industries Corporation Ltd.
http://www.artclay.co.jp/htm
Distributors/Agencies
http://www.artclay.co.jp/htm/family

Others

㉞ Mini Pan

Used as a metal dish when firing silver clay on a portable stove.

㉟ Stainless steel mesh cover

Used to cover a clay piece on the pan when firing on a portable stove.

㊱ Shrinkage stopper

Used to stop a silver clay ring from shrinking during firing.

㊲ Ceramic tape

A heat-resistant buffer, used by winding around the shrinkage stopper.

㊳ Ceramic wool

An insulating material to adjust temperature (not used in this book).

㊴ Metal tongs

Used to remove the Mini Pan from the stove.

explore more beautiful polymer clay projects

with these innovative resources from Interweave

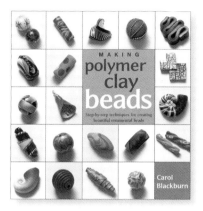

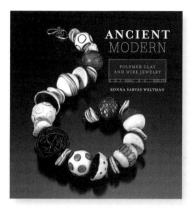

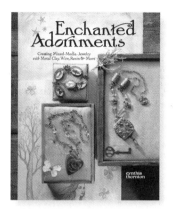

Making Polymer Clay Beads
Step-by-Step Techniques
for Creating Beautiful
Ornamental Beads

Carol Blackburn
ISBN 978-1-59668-019-7
$24.95

Ancient Modern
Polymer Clay and Wire Jewelry
Ronna Sarvas Weltman
ISBN 978-1-59668-097-5
$22.95

Enchanted Adornments
Creating Mixed-Media Jewelry
with Metal Clay, Wire,
Resin & More

Cynthia Thornton
ISBN 978-1-59668-157-6
$24.95

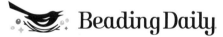

Are you Beading Daily?

Check out *Jewelry Artist,* a trusted guide to the art of gems, jewelry making, design, beads, clays, minerals, and more. Whether you are a beginner, an experienced artisan, or in the jewelry business, *Jewelry Artist* can take you to a whole new level. Jewelryartistmagazine.com

Stringing, wirework, stitching, knotting, weaving, embroidery, beadmaking—it's all a part of *Beading Daily,* Interweave's online community. A free e-newsletter, free beading projects, a daily blog, tips and techniques, new product announcements, event news, galleries, and interviews are just some of the treats that await you. Whether you're just getting started or already live to bead, there's a place for you at *Beading Daily.* Sign up at beadingdaily.com.

 Jewelry Making Daily *Shop*

shop.jewelrymaking.com

 Beading Daily SHOP

shop.beadingdaily.com

Rie Nagumo

Born in Tokyo, she graduated from Tokyo Zokei University majoring in Textile Design, and worked as an in-house designer for major companies in charge of textile or jewelry design. After studying design in Italy, she established the Rie Design Studio in Tokyo in 2002. Presently she is active in planning jewelry-making products, as well as design and production of jewelry as a freelance jewelry designer, while also acting as an instructor for various jewelry classes.
http://www.riedesign.jp

Other publications:
Accessories with White Porcelain and Fine Silver Clay (Nihon Vogue-sha Co., Ltd.)
Silver accessories by Rie Nagumo (Ondori Co., Ltd.)

Editorial supervision:
Silver Ring Design (Ondori Co., Ltd.)
Fine Silver Work by Men (Gakken Holdings Co., Ltd.)

Materials contributed by:
STAEDTLER Mars GmbH & Co. KG.
Mitsubishi Materials Corporation
Craft House